William Heinemann Ltd Michelin House
81 Fulham Road London SW3 6RB

LONDON MELBOURNE AUCKLAND

First Published 1989 by William Heinemann
Copyright © 1989 Bettina Paterson
ISBN 434 95611 2

Produced by Proost International Book Production
Printed and bound in Belgium

Wild Animals

Bettina Paterson

HEINEMANN · LONDON

brown bear

orang utan

camel

crocodile

polar bear

penguins

giraffe

rhinoceros

zebra

leopard

gorilla

buffalo

whale

koala

elephant

walrus

hippopotamus

parrot

tiger

panda

kangaroo

seal

llama